# Opposites:

# Front and Back

Luana K. Mitten

Rourke

**Publishing LLC**
Vero Beach, Florida 32964

www.rourkepublishing.com

PHOTO CREDITS: © Jani Bryson: page 3 right; © Alexander Shalamov: page 3 left; © RichVintage: page 6, 7; © Eddy Lund: page 21 top; © Rick Sargeant: page 21 bottom;  © Brian Sak: page 22, 23

Editor: Kelli Hicks

Cover design by Nicola Stratford, bdpublishing.com

Interior Design by Heather Botto

Spanish Editorial Services by Cambridge BrickHouse, Inc.   www.cambridgebh.com

**Library of Congress Cataloging-in-Publication Data**

Mitten, Luana K.
  Opposites : front and back / Luana K. Mitten.
     p. cm. --  (Concepts)
  Learning the concept of opposites through riddles and poetry.
  ISBN 978-1-60472-418-9 (hardcover)
  ISBN 978-1-60472-814-9 (softcover)
  ISBN 978-1-60472-500-1 (hardcover bilingual)
  ISBN 978-1-60694-790-6 (softcover bilingual)
  1.  English language--Synonyms and antonyms--Juvenile literature. 2.  Riddles, Juvenile. I. Title.
  PE1591M644 2008
  423'.1--dc22
                              2008018798

Printed in the USA
CG/CG

Rourke Publishing

www.rourkepublishing.com – rourke@rourkepublishing.com
Post Office Box 3328, Vero Beach, FL 32964

Front and back, back and front, what's the difference between front and back?

I have one wheel in the front and two wheels in the back. What am I?

5

A tricycle

back

front

I have one wheel in the front and one wheel in the back. What am I?

A  motorcycle

front

11

back

I have doors in the front and a hatchback in the rear. What am I?

A car

back

14

front

15

I have doors in the front and a bed in the back. What am I?

17

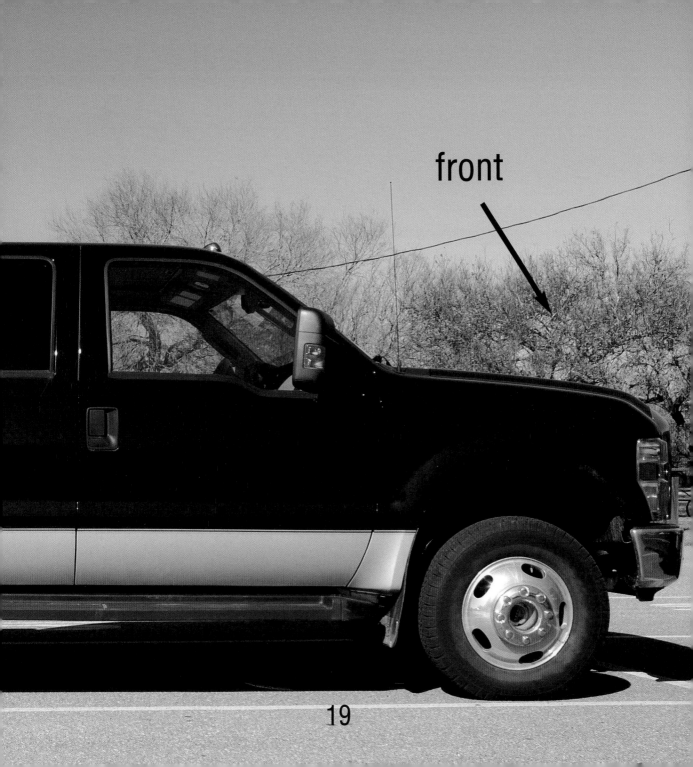

front

I have an engine in the front and a caboose in the back. What am I?

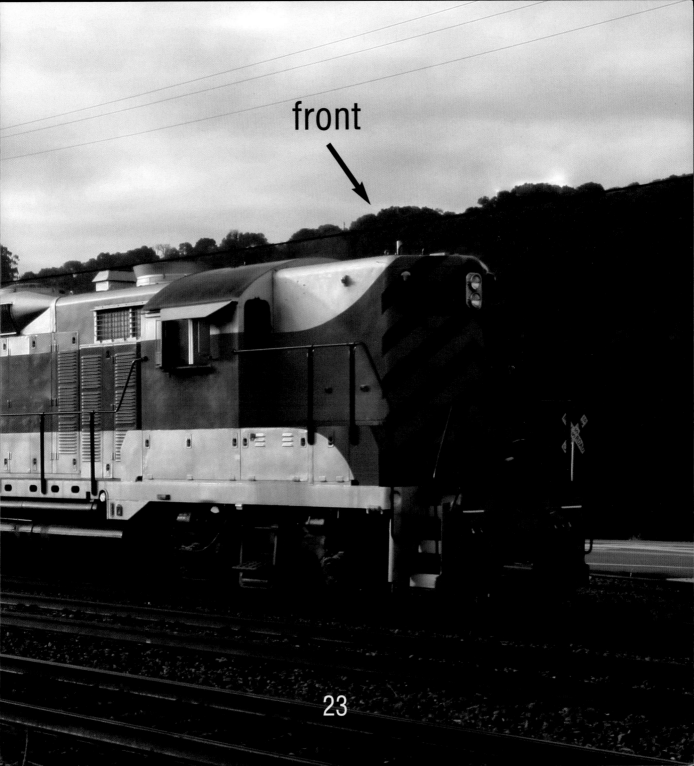

front

# Index

back    3, 4, 6, 8, 11, 12, 14,
    16, 18, 20, 22
car    14
front    3, 4, 7, 8, 10, 12, 15,
    16, 19, 20, 22, 23

motorcycle    10
pickup truck    18
train    22
tricycle    6

## Further Reading

Child, Lauren. *Charlie and Lola's Opposites.* 2007.
Ford, Bernette. Sorrentino, Christiano. *A Big Dog: An Opposites Book,* 2008.
Falk, Laine. *Let's Talk About Opposites: Morning to Night,* 2007.
Holland, Gina. *Soft and Hard (I Know My Opposites),* 2007.

## Recommended Websites

www.abcteach.com/grammar/online/opposites1.htm
www.resources.kaboose.com/games/read1html
www.learn4good.com/kids/preschool_english_spanish_language_books.htm

## About the Author

Luana Mitten and her family live in Tampa, Florida where they like riding in the front or back cars of all the nearby roller coasters.